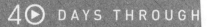
40 DAYS THROUGH

1 & 2 THESSALONIANS

A WORLD-CHANGING FAITH

SIX-SESSION STUDY GUIDE

LEVI LUSKO

WITH KEVIN & SHERRY HARNEY

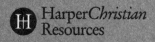

HarperChristian
Resources

40 Days Through the Book: 1 & 2 Thessalonians Study Guide
© 2021 by Levi Lusko

Requests for information should be addressed to: HarperChristian Resources, *3900 Sparks Dr. SE, Grand Rapids, Michigan 49546*

ISBN 978-0-310-12743-7 (softcover)
ISBN 978-0-310-13113-7 (ebook)

HarperChristian Resources titles may be purchased in bulk for church, business, fundraising, or ministry use. For information, please e-mail ResourceSpecialist@ChurchSource.com.

The themes of this study are drawn from the video study of the same name by Levi Lusko. All other resources, including the session introductions, small group discussion questions, prayer direction, and the 40 Days learning and reflection exercises, have been written by Kevin and Sherry Harney in collaboration with Levi Lusko.

First printing May 2021 / Printed in the United States of America

CONTENTS

How to Use This Guide v

Introduction to 1 and 2 Thessalonians ix

SESSION 1: **THE WORD IS OUT** (1 THESSALONIANS 1:1–10) 1

SESSION 2: **NEVER GIVE UP** (1 THESSALONIANS 2:1–16) 19

SESSION 3: **BORN FOR THIS** (1 THESSALONIANS 3:1–13) 35

SESSION 4: **MIND YOUR BUSINESS** (1 THESSALONIANS 4:1–12) 51

SESSION 5: **BETWEEN NOW AND THEN** (1 THESSALONIANS 5:12–28) . . 69

SESSION 6: **KEEP CALM AND CARRY ON** (2 THESSALONIANS) 87

Leader's Guide 103

HOW TO USE THIS GUIDE

SCOPE AND SEQUENCE

Welcome to the *40 Days Through the Book* study on 1 and 2 Thessalonians! During the course of the next six weeks, you and your fellow group members will embark on an in-depth exploration of the apostle Paul's message to the believers in that part of the Mediterranean world. During this study, you will learn approximately when he wrote the books, the audience for whom he wrote, and the background and context in which they were written. But, more importantly, through the teaching by Levi Lusko, you will explore the key themes that Paul relates in these books—and how his teachings relate to you today.

SESSION OUTLINE

The *40 Days Through the Book* video study is designed to be experienced in a group setting (such as a Bible study, Sunday school class, or small group gathering) and also as an individual study. Each session begins with an introduction reading and question. You will then watch a video with Levi Lusko, which can be accessed via the streaming code found on the inside front cover. There is an outline provided in the guide for you to take notes and gather your reflections as you watch the video.

Next, you will engage in a time of directed discussion, review the memory verses for the week, and then close each session with a time of personal reflection and prayer. (Note that if your group is larger, you may wish to watch the videos together and then break into smaller groups of four to six people, to ensure that everyone has time to participate in discussions.)

40-DAY JOURNEY

What is truly unique about this study, and all of the other studies in the *40 Days Through the Book* series, are the daily learning resources that will lead you into a deeper engagement with the text. Each week, you will be given a set of daily readings, with accompanying reflection questions, to help you explore the material that you covered during your group time.

The first day's reading will focus on the key verse to memorize for the week. In the other weekly readings, you will be invited to read a passage from 1 or 2 Thessalonians, reflect on the text, and then respond with some guided journal questions. On the final day, you will review the key verse again and recite it from memory. As you work through the six weeks' worth of material in this section, you will read (and, in some cases, reread) the entire books of 1 and 2 Thessalonians.

Now, you may be wondering why you will be doing this over the course of *forty* days. Certainly, there is nothing special about that number. But there is something biblical about it. In the Bible, the number forty typically designates a time of *testing*. The great flood in Noah's time lasted forty days. Moses lived forty years in Egypt and another forty years in the desert before he led God's people. He spent forty days on Mount Sinai receiving God's laws and sent spies, for forty days, to investigate the land of Canaan. Later, God sent the prophet Jonah to warn ancient Nineveh, for forty days, that its destruction would come because of the people's sins.

Even more critically, in the New Testament we read that Jesus spent forty days in the wilderness, fasting and praying. It marked a critical transition point in his ministry—the place where he set about to fulfill the mission that God had intended. During this time Jesus was tested relentlessly by the enemy . . . and prevailed. When he returned to Galilee, he was a different person than the man who had entered into the wilderness forty days before. The same will be true for you as you commit to this forty-day journey through 1 and 2 Thessalonians.

GROUP FACILITATION

You and your fellow group members should have your own copy of this study guide. Not only will this help you engage when your group is meeting, but it will also allow you to fully enter into the *40 Days* learning experience. Keep in mind the video, questions, and activities are simply tools to help you engage with the session. The real power and life-transformation will come as you dig into the Scriptures and seek to live out the truths you learn along the way.

Finally, you will need to appoint a leader or facilitator for the group who is responsible for starting the video teaching and for keeping track of time during discussions and activities. Leaders may also read questions aloud and monitor discussions, prompting participants to respond and ensuring that everyone has the opportunity to participate. For more thorough instructions on this role, see the Leader's Guide included at the back of this guide.

INTRODUCTION

1 AND 2 THESSALONIANS

AUTHOR, DATE, AND LOCATION

The letters to God's people in the church in Thessalonica were written by Paul, the Pastor. First and Second Thessalonians came from deep within his pastoral heart. Although there are clear theological underpinnings, Paul's primary focus in these letters is how we should live more than a deep exposition of what we are to believe. These profoundly personal letters were written around AD 50–52 and address what it looks like to live as a Christian. These letters were written to real-life people living in the largest city in Macedonia. This capital city was at the crossroads of the world. Positioned on the Via Egnatia and Thermic Gulf (both travel and trade routes), Thessalonica was a center of culture, religion (of every sort), and trade.

THE BIG PICTURE

When Paul and his ministry companions arrived in the city of Thessalonica, they came battered, bruised, and weary. They had just been in Philippi and had been stripped, flogged, beaten with rods, and thrown into prison. After being miraculously set free from jail and leading a revival meeting with the jailer and his family, they moved on (see Acts 16:16–40). The next stop was Thessalonica (see Acts 17:1–9).

Rather than find a quiet place to lick his wounds and have a little "me time," Paul went right to the synagogue in Thessalonica and for three weeks in a row he preached the message of Jesus the Messiah. By the grace of God and through the power of the Holy Spirit, some Jews became Jesus followers and many Greeks who were spiritually hungry also came to faith in the Savior.

Once again, conflict arose, mobs incited violence, and the Christians in the city packed up Paul and his ministry companions and sent them on to Berea. They were only in Thessalonica for a couple of months, but Paul fell in love with the people in this fresh new Jesus community.

What happened next is staggering and beautiful! It stands as an example for all Christians, in all places, at all times. The believers in the city of Thessalonica fell so in love with Jesus and followed the Savior with such passion, that word of their faith began to spread from city to city. Paul would show up in a new region to do ministry and the people there were already talking about how the Thessalonian believers had warmly welcomed Paul and his companions, how they had rejected idols and embraced the true and living

God, and how their lives were focused fully on Jesus (see 1 Thessalonians 1:7–10).

In response, Paul was inspired by the Holy Spirit to write two short, power-packed letters to this group of passionate Jesus followers. The first letter is only 89 verses. The second is 47 verses. Think about it, Psalm 119 is 150 verses long. The two letters to the Thessalonian church are only 136 verses combined. Yet, Paul addresses many of the core beliefs and practices Christians of all maturity levels need to know about to honor Jesus and impact the world.

The books of 1 and 2 Thessalonians stand out as deeply pastoral and practical for all believers. If you want to remember what really matters about faith in Jesus and hear the call to follow Jesus on your daily adventure of faith, these books will propel you forward on your journey.

EPIC THEMES

There are several themes in 1 and 2 Thessalonians that are worthy of our focus. Some of these include:

- **The power of an effective witness.** Be a faithful and passionate follower of Jesus and the world will see and be impacted (1 Thessalonians chapter 1 and 2 Thessalonians chapter 1).
- **God delights in resilient faith.** Stand strong in your faith and hang in there, even when things get tough (1 Thessalonians chapter 2 and 2 Thessalonians chapter 2).

- **Keep the gospel of Jesus central . . . always.** There are many things that matter, but at the center of our faith and lives should be the good news of Jesus (1 Thessalonians chapter 2).
- **Live with Christian love, care, and family tenderness.** We should be concerned for the well-being of others. Of all the commandments, Jesus was clear that loving people should always be central to who we are and what we do (1 Thessalonians chapter 3).
- **Let Jesus be Lord of all.** Follow Jesus and live for him in every part of your life. This is what it means to be his follower (1 Thessalonians chapter 4 and 2 Thessalonians chapter 3).
- **This life is not the end of the story.** Jesus will come again! So, we are to live for our Savior every day and be ready to see him face to face for eternity (1 Thessalonians chapters 4 and 5 and 2 Thessalonians chapter 2).

Thessalonica was positioned on major trade routes—a cultural center and a hub of all sorts of religious activity. If the good news of Jesus could take root in this place, it would spread across the known world. There were travelers in and out of this region daily and they were headed to the ends of the earth . . . literally! The simple truths that God taught these believers through the letters of 1 and 2 Thessalonians were world-changing. They still are! These same truths can transform your life and continue through you to impact people all over your world.

THE WORD IS OUT

1 THESSALONIANS 1:1–10

*When we encounter Jesus, the Messiah,
everything changes. When our lives are transformed
by the power of the Savior, people notice, the word
gets out, and the good news spreads.*

WELCOME

What does it take for the word to get out? How fast does news spread? At the speed of thought, the typing of a message, and the hitting of a send button. In a world of social media and instant global communication, the word gets out in about thirty seconds.

Good news, bad news, world updates, personal secrets, accurate or inaccurate, news spreads faster than wildfire! It has not always been this way. Just a few short decades ago, people used phones as a primary means of communication, and they would pass on information to one person at a time. Before that, they sent letters that were hand sorted and delivered days later. The word would get out, but it was much slower. If the average person wanted to get the word on newsworthy stories and topics, they had to wait until evening and turn on their television so they could hear a news anchor report on the day's stories.

In the ancient world of the New Testament, getting the word out was very difficult. No phones, no computers, no TV, no social media. Communication happened person to person and most of it was verbal. A vast part of the population did not read, and the cost of writing materials was high. Even if a letter was written, it had to be hand carried from one place to another. In the days of the apostle Paul, news traveled exceedingly slow.

What was staggering about the church in the city of Thessalonica is that in a world with no social media, phones, or postal services, the word about their faith and love for Jesus moved faster than the apostle Paul could travel. It seemed that everywhere he went, the story of their bold and deep faith got there first.

Imagine if this were to happen to you and your church. What if the story of your church and your personal faith was spreading all over your city, county, and state? What story would be told? What themes would emerge? If someone were to post pictures and stories about how you live for Jesus, would that be a good thing? Would the world be inspired by your example? Would your life of faith draw people to Jesus and bring glory to his name?

SHARE

If someone secretly followed you around for a week and took pictures of what you did and recorded what you said, what are some of the positive things they could tell others to get the word out on your life? What would they see that points to the presence, power, and beauty of Jesus?

WATCH

Play the video for session one. As you watch, use the following outline to record any thoughts, questions, or key points that stand out to you.

A powerful overview of the Christian journey

1 and 2 Thessalonians is for everyone . . . for both the new believer and the mature follower of Jesus

Meeting Levi, his family, and a dog named Tabasco

The **Why**: The word was out

The **Who**: Paul and his ministry team

The **First Connection**: Affirmation and Correction

The **Second Connection**: Communication and Demonstration

The Third Connection: Tribulation and Jubilation

The Fourth and Final Connection: Reception and Transmission

DISCUSS

Take a few minutes with your group members to discuss what you just watched and explore these concepts in Scripture. Use the following questions to help guide your discussion.

1. What impacted you the most as you watched Levi's teaching on 1 Thessalonians 1:1–10?

2. What are signs that we are growing in faith, love, and hope? Which of these three characteristics has been strongest in your life over the past month and how do you see this attribute growing?

What are indicators that a person's faith, love, and hope are waning and need to be rekindled? Which of these three needs more attention in your own life and what is one step you can take to increase it?

3. **Read 1 Thessalonians 1:4–7.** Tell about a person in your life who has clearly communicated the message of the Bible to you. Share one lesson you have learned from this person who models what it looks like to embrace the beauty of God's truth. How are you seeking to follow the example of this person and teach the message of the Bible to another person?

4. Describe different ways God pricks our heart, holds up a mirror for us to see something wrong, or wakes us up to an area of much needed growth. Why do you think God does this? Tell about a time God did this in the past or how he is doing it right now. What does God want to transform in you, and how can your group members be part of this journey of growth?

5. **Read 1 Thessalonians 1:6–10.** Describe, in your own words, what the people around the ancient world were saying about the Christians in the Thessalonian church. What would it mean in your community today if everyone was saying the same sorts of things about you and the members of your congregation?

6. Tell about a person who you long to come to faith in Jesus. How can your group members support you and inspire you in your journey of gospel transmission to this person?

MEMORIZE

Each session, you will be given a key verse from the passage covered in the video teaching to memorize. This week, your memory verse is 1 Thessalonians 1:3:

> *We remember before our God and Father your work produced by faith, your labor prompted by love, and your endurance inspired by hope in our Lord Jesus Christ.*

Have everyone recite this verse out loud. Ask for any volunteers who would like to say the verse from memory.

RESPOND

What will you take away from this session? What is one practical next step you can take to carry the love and truth of Jesus to the unique places you go in the flow of a normal week?

PRAY

Close your group time by praying in any of the following directions:

- Thank God for the people in your life who have lived as an example of mature faith.

- Ask God to help you live in a way that communicates the love and good news of Jesus and that also demonstrates the love and grace of Jesus.
- Pray for your group members to experience deep and lasting joy, even in times of tribulation.
- Lift up a prayer for one person in your personal circle who really needs to receive the gospel of Jesus. Offer yourself to God and invite him to use you to share Jesus naturally with this person.

SESSION ONE

Reflect on the material you have covered in this session by engaging in the following between-session learning resources. Each week, you will begin by reviewing the key verse to memorize for the session. During the next five days, you will have an opportunity to read a portion of 1 and 2 Thessalonians, reflect on what you learn, respond by taking action, journal some of your insights, and pray about what God has taught you. Finally, the last day, you will review the key verse and reflect on what you have learned for the week.

DAY 1

Memorize: Begin this week's personal study by reciting 1 Thessalonians 1:3:

> *We remember before our God and Father your work produced by faith, your labor prompted by love, and your endurance inspired by hope in our Lord Jesus Christ.*

Now try to say the verse from memory.

Reflect: Take time throughout the day to take note of your words, actions, attitudes, motives. Pay special attention to where your faith is alive and active. Think about what people see and might be saying about you and your faith. Be humble and honest. Without being prideful, what are ways you can let your faith in Jesus be noticed by the people you encounter in a normal day?

DAY 2

Read: 1 Thessalonians 1–2.

Reflect: We can speak well of other believers and local churches. Take time this week to learn about a church in your community (other than the one you attend). Browse their website. You may want to ask a friend or neighbor about the church they attend and what they love about their church family and the ministry of their church. Then, make a point of telling others (in your church, other churches, or even non-believers) about the good things you have heard about that church. Get the word out and bless that church. You might even write a note to their pastor and thank them for their ministry.

Journal:

- List ways you could affirm and celebrate the lives of Christians you know. Be specific and be sure these are doable and practical. Also, include one action you can take to get out the good word.
- What keeps you from affirming other people and churches? What can you do to overcome this obstacle?

Pray: Ask God for eyes to see the good things in other believers and churches. Then, pray for the Holy Spirit to give you courage to speak well of this person or church in public settings.

DAY 3

Read: 1 Thessalonians 3–4.

Reflect: Use your journal space below to make a list of three Christians you know who are really seeking to follow Jesus. Next to their names, write one or two positive behaviors or actions you see in their lives. Then, send them a text, email, or call to affirm them for being a wonderful example for you and others.

Journal:

- List of behaviors you see in mature Christians that inspire you to be more like Jesus.
- Write a prayer asking God to infuse you with Holy Spirit power to adopt one of these behaviors for yourself.

Pray: Ask God to give you courage to regularly and consistently affirm the people in your life. Pray for eyes to see the good examples of others and adopt these God-honoring practices in your own life.

DAY 4

Read: 1 Thessalonians 5.

Reflect: Make an effort to align your words and your actions. Look for times you say something but fail to act on it. Christians are notorious for saying things like, "I'll pray for you," and then they forget to pray. If this happens to you, consider one of these solutions: (1) Don't say, "I'll pray for you." Instead, say, "May I pray for you right now?" Then, do it. (2) If you say you will pray, stop right then and there, and add a daily reminder on your phone so you have a pop-up every day for a week. (3) The minute you have open time following the encounter when you promised to pray, carve out a few minutes to lift up the need you promised to pray for.

Pick one area of your life where there is no alignment between words and actions and make a plan to correct it.

Journal:
- Write down the area you want to work on aligning your words and actions.
- Write down two or three ways you can take a practical step to make this alignment.

Pray: Ask God to open your eyes to see where your words and actions need to be consistent.

DAY 5

Read: 2 Thessalonians 1.

Reflect: Read Acts 16:16–40 and study the situation and attitudes of Paul and Silas. Read Philippians 4:4–7 and reflect on how these words relate to a situation such as the one Paul faced in Acts 16. Think about how you respond to hard times and what happens to your joy quotient in these difficult situations.

Journal:
- Write down your thoughts as you read Acts 16:16–40 and Philippians 4:4–7.
- Take note of how you tend to respond in hard times and how much joy (or lack of joy) you have when times are tough.

Pray: Ask God to help you keep your eyes on him and your heart joyful in the tough times of life. Pray for people you love who are going through painful situations right now. Ask the Holy Spirit of the Living God to breathe joy into their heart and lives.

DAY 6

Read: 2 Thessalonians 2–3.

Reflect: We all know people (family members, friends, neighbors, coworkers . . .) who have never received the amazing grace of Jesus. Take time to pray for each one, asking God to open their heart to the prompting and invitation of the Spirit.

Journal:
- Write the names of three to five people you know who are not yet followers of Jesus.
- Make a list of simple and practical ways you can serve them in the name of Jesus: pray for them, make a meal or do some other act of kindness for them, seek to share what your relationship with Jesus means to you.

Pray: Ask God to give you the right words and courage to have a spiritual conversation with at least one person that you write about in the journal section above.

DAY 7

Memorize: Conclude this week's personal study by again reciting 1 Thessalonians 1:3:

> *We remember before our God and Father your work produced by faith, your labor prompted by love, and your endurance inspired by hope in our Lord Jesus Christ.*

Reflect: Our words have power. More power than most of us recognize. Take ten minutes to review your recent texts and emails that are personal in nature. Honestly and humbly ask yourself if your words are thoughtful and gracious. Or, are they sharp and harsh? In the coming days, seek to be as gracious and kind as you can with your words—both written and spoken—while still communicating what needs to be said.

NEVER GIVE UP

1 THESSALONIANS 2:1–16

A world-changing faith will always face resistance and opposition. This was true in the first century and it is just as true today. Faithful followers of Jesus must learn to stand strong, push forward, and never give up. As we hang in there, God holds on to us.

WELCOME

January 19 is a significant and important date.

The experience that occurs on this day every year is sad and shocking. It happens to millions of people and they don't even know it. What happens on January 19 damages families, businesses, friendships, and individuals all over the world. In a study of over 800 million activities, researchers have learned that most people give up their New Year's resolutions around

January 19. They quit! Of course, this date is an average . . . some quit earlier, and others hang in there a bit longer before they throw in the towel. The point is that many people abandon their goals and commitments less than three weeks after they start. We could call January 19, "Global Giving-Up-Day."

"I am going to exercise four mornings a week and eat more healthy food this year." January 19 is the day the gym membership becomes a poor investment and the new juicer on the kitchen counter starts colleting cobwebs. "I'm going to read my Bible each morning and journal a few insights and prayers." By January 19 the snooze button replaces the early alarm and the prayer journal becomes a decoration on the nightstand. "I'm going to turn off the TV a few evenings a week and have conversations with my spouse and kids . . . maybe we'll start playing some board games and read together . . . it is going to be amazing!" Three weeks later media consumption is back in full swing and everyone is binging on streaming shows on their own device and in separate rooms.

Giving up is easy! When things get tough, the natural response is to quit. It is the path of least resistance. It is a smooth, simple, downhill slope.

It is also deadly!

We will never know the things that could have been done in our world if people had refused to give up. We can't calculate the glorious impact on our lives and the lives of others if we would have pressed on when things got tough. What we can do is look around and see the amazing things that happen when people refuse to give up. Dreams come true. Marriages are restored. Friendships are healed. Churches grow. Ministries thrive. Holiness deepens. Faith explodes. The world is changed!

SHARE

Tell about a difficult and painful time you refused to give up but really hung in there. What came to pass that would never have happened if you had given up?

WATCH

Play the video for session two. As you watch, use the following outline to record any thoughts, questions, or key points that stand out to you.

Never give in and never give up

The context of 1 Thessalonians . . . a moment ripe for giving up

A real-life story of hanging in there

Lessons from the apostle Paul

1. Never give up . . . even when things don't seem to be working

2. Never give up . . . even when people misunderstand your motives

3. Never give up . . . even when it's hard

Benefits from being tenacious and hanging in there

1. The Word of God was received

2. The Word of God was spread

3. The strength to face roadblocks

DISCUSS

Take a few minutes with your group members to discuss what you just watched and explore these concepts in Scripture. Use the following questions to help guide your discussion.

1. What impacted you the most as you watched Levi's teaching on 1 Thessalonians 2?

2. What are some of the things in our culture and world that people seem to be giving up on and what are some of the potential consequences if this continues?

3. What are some specific areas of calling and conviction that God wants every one of his followers to be sure they never give up on?

4. **Read 1 Thessalonians 2:1–2 and 2 Corinthians 11:23–28.** What were some of the things the apostle Paul faced in his ministry that could have made him say, "This is just not working out the way I would have planned it?"

5. Sometimes God calls us to live and function in ways that don't seem to pay off or bear fruit immediately, but he calls us to press on. What are some examples of actions, behaviors, or attitudes that don't align with the current "norms and practices" in our world? Why is it so important for Christians to keep living and thinking in godly and biblical ways even when we don't see the results we might hope for?

6. Tell about a season when you were following Jesus and working very hard, but you found yourself either:
    ○ discouraged because things didn't seem to be working as they should
    ○ misunderstood or misrepresented
    ○ exhausted

What helped you to keep pressing on? What kept you focused on Jesus despite the challenges you encountered?

How can you encourage and pray for your group members who may need encouragement at this moment in time?

MEMORIZE

Each session, you will be given a key verse from the passage covered in the video teaching to memorize. This week, your memory verse is 1 Thessalonians 2:4:

> . . . We speak as those approved by God to be entrusted with the gospel. We are not trying to please people but God, who tests our hearts.

Have everyone recite this verse out loud. Ask for any volunteers who would like to say the verse from memory.

RESPOND

What will you take away from this session? What is one practical next step you can take to stand strong and not give up in an area of life that is very difficult? How can your group members pray for you and encourage you as you stand strong?

PRAY

Close your group time by praying in any of the following directions:

- Thank God for the people he has placed in your life who have modeled what it looks like to follow Jesus through the hard times and stay faithful even when things get tough.
- Ask the Holy Spirit to fill members of your group with power and strength to never give up, even when they are facing pain, loss, and struggle in their lives.
- Pray for the comfort and care of Jesus to fill the lives of people you know who are feeling the painful impact of others giving up on them.
- Ask God to give you courage to press on and keep following him even when the world pushes back and people don't understand why you follow Jesus the way you do.

SESSION TWO

Reflect on the material you have covered in this session by engaging in the following between-session learning resources. Each week, you will begin by reviewing the key verse to memorize for the session. During the next five days, you will have an opportunity to read a portion of 1 and 2 Thessalonians and reflect on what you learn, respond by taking action, journal some of your insights, and pray about what God has taught you. Finally, the last day, you will review the key verse and reflect on what you have learned for the week.

DAY 8

Memorize: Begin this week's personal study by reciting 1 Thessalonians 2:4:

> . . . We speak as those approved by God to be entrusted with the gospel. We are not trying to please people but God, who tests our hearts.

Now try to say the verse from memory.

Reflect: The apostle Paul and his companions had been treated badly and refused to stop sharing the gospel even when there was significant opposition to their ministry. Think about an area of life you are seeking to follow or serve Jesus. What is getting in the way? How are you being discouraged? What can you do to keep pressing on as you seek to please God and make sure you don't give up?

DAY 9

Read: 1 Thessalonians 1 and 2 (especially focus on 1 Thessalonians 2:1–2).

Reflect: Suffering and hardship are real! Even when we are following Jesus and being faithful to his call, we can suffer. This was true for the apostle Paul and his ministry companions; it was true for some of the most faithful people in the Bible; it was true for Jesus; and it will be true for us. Think about these words, "Outrageous suffering!" That is what we read about in this passage. Faithful servants of Jesus were being persecuted and treated terribly. Here is the astounding thing . . . they did not give up! They kept following God's leadership even when times were hard. Reflect about times when you have suffered, pressed on, and seen God do something wonderful. How can you encourage other Christians to hang in there and never give up on following Jesus?

Journal:
- How has God been with you and watched over you in a time of struggle and suffering that continued over time?
- What can you do to fortify yourself and prepare yourself to stand strong in the hard times of life?

Pray: Thank God for being near you, even in the hard times of life. Ask for eyes to see his presence and power in the tough days.

DAY 10

Read: 1 Thessalonians 3 and 1 Thessalonians 2:3–6.

Reflect: The driving force in the life of a Christian should be to please God in all things. We get off track when we care more about what other people think of us than what God sees. Paul and his ministry partners were committed to please God above all and avoid behaviors and life patterns that were about putting people above God. When are you tempted to make the focus of your life about pleasing people and making them happy (above God)?

Journal:
- What are times and situations you have given in to the temptation to please people more than God?
- What can you do to make sure God is your first audience and that honoring him is the driving force of your life?

Pray: Thank God that he always has his eyes on you and that he delights when your desire is to honor him. Confess those times you have been living in ways that seek to please people more than the One who made you and loves you most.

DAY 11

Read: 1 Thessalonians 4 and 5 and 1 Thessalonians 2:7–9.

Reflect: Tenderness, care, and compassion should mark the life of every follower of Jesus. Paul and his ministry team described themselves as caring with the heart and actions of a nursing mother. Can you imagine a more tender picture than a mother of a newborn caring for her little one? This is an image of service that is willing to give everything, including life! Who has cared for you and helped nurture your Christian faith with tenderness and kindness?

Journal:
- What can you learn from people in your life who show the tenderness of a mother with her newborn baby?
- How can you increase the care you extend to others (be specific about what you can do to show deeper levels of compassion and tenderness)?

Pray: Thank God for the people he has placed in your life who are an example of compassion and care (to you or others).

DAY 12

Read: 2 Thessalonians 1 and 1 Thessalonians 2:10–12.

Reflect: Not only were Paul and his team of ministry partners like a mother, but they also cared like a father. Like a dad who cheers on a child learning a new skill, they cheered on the Thessalonian Christians to never give up, keep pressing on, and to be fearless as they followed Jesus. Consider someone God has placed in your life who has raised the bar for you and really challenged you to keep taking steps forward in faith.

Journal:

- How have people challenged you to stand strong in faith and keep following the Savior boldly?
- How can God use you to encourage and urge others to follow Jesus with new passion and serve him with a relentless commitment?

Pray: Thank God for the people he has placed in your life who encourage, challenge, and call you to greater faith and faithfulness.

DAY 13

Read: 2 Thessalonians 2–3 and 1 Thessalonians 2:13–16.

Reflect: The Word of God changes lives! When the people in Thessalonica recognized that God was speaking to them, they responded. We have the staggering privilege of having the Scriptures available in print, audio, and right on our phone or other devices. It has never been easier to learn from the Bible. How can you go deeper into the Scriptures and make them an even more important part of your daily life?

Journal:
- What habits, disciplines, or patterns have you established that help you engage with the text and truth of the Bible?
- What are a couple of ways you can increase your biblical engagement and find greater joy in learning from the Scriptures?

Pray: Pray for discipline and commitment to go deeper into the Bible in the coming weeks.

DAY 14

Memorize: Conclude this week's personal study by again reciting 1 Thessalonians 2:4:

> . . . *We speak as those approved by God to be entrusted with the gospel. We are not trying to please people but God, who tests our hearts.*

Reflect: It is possible to stand strong, follow Jesus in times of opposition, and keep living for him. Reflect back over the past seven days. How have you been encouraged to keep following Jesus? What are ways the enemy has enticed you to give up in the past and how can you take action to be sure you keep pressing on as you go forward?

BORN FOR THIS

___

1 THESSALONIANS 3:1–13

When we have a purpose from God, we gain a heavenly perspective and God fills us with fresh power. Each of us has unique giftings and callings that make us who we are. In the book of 1 Thessalonians, we discover that there are also some things that every Christian is born for.

WELCOME

Usain Bolt has eight gold medals for sprinting. He won the 100-meter sprint and the 200-meter sprint in three consecutive Olympics. No other runner in history has accomplished this staggering feat. Usain is the eleven-time world champion of the 100-meter sprint, the 200-meter sprint, and the 4x4 100-meter relay for seven consecutive years from 2009 to 2015. You might say that Usain was born to run! Of course, he trained hard and gave much of his life to accomplish all he did, but there was also something in the way God made him that gave Usain an advantage as a runner.

Wolfgang Amadeus Mozart began composing musical pieces at the age of five. He wrote more than 600 works, and many of them are still loved, performed, and enjoyed to this day. His life was cut short in 1791 when he died at only thirty-five years old. Just do the math. If he began composing at five and died thirty years later, he had to write an average of twenty original compositions a year. It is easy to see that Mozart was born to be a composer.

Albert Einstein was born to think. Amelia Earhart was born to fly. Serena Williams was born to play tennis. Billy Graham was born to share the good news of Jesus. You get the picture. Some people have a purpose that draws them irresistibly to fulfill who they were born to be.

In the life of every person mentioned there is a story of how they made a decision to follow their calling and pursue their purpose. Along with God-given ability each person needs to exercise their own volition and step into their destiny.

When a person comes to faith in Jesus, they have a calling, a purpose, a reason for living. We don't get to define what it will be. Our Creator God declares it. What we get to do is partner with God in discovering and following that purpose. There is nothing more exciting, nothing more challenging, and nothing more meaningful than learning what we were born for and going after it with all our might!

SHARE

When you became a follower of Jesus, what did you learn about God's plan and purpose for your life? How have you partnered with God to live into what you were born for?

WATCH

Play the video for session three. As you watch, use the following outline to record any thoughts, questions, or key points that stand out to you.

When you have a purpose, it gives perspective that allows you to tap into God's power

Paul knew his purpose

Paul was like both a mother and a father

The relationship of Paul and Timothy

You were born for . . . **adversity** (1 Thessalonians 3:1–4)

God is sovereign in the midst of our struggles

God's refining power is available in hard times

You were born for . . . **affection** (1 Thessalonians 3:5–11)

You were born for . . . **progress** (1 Thessalonians 3:1–13)

DISCUSS

Take a few minutes with your group members to discuss what you just watched and explore these concepts in Scripture. Use the following questions to help guide your discussion.

I. What impacted you the most as you watched Levi's teaching on 1 Thessalonians 3?

2. How have you experienced gaining a clear purpose that adjusted your perspective and gave you power to live the way God has designed you to live?

3. **Read 1 Thessalonians 3:1–4.** Paul writes about Christians being destined for trials and being prepared for persecution. Tell about a refining time in your life and how you experienced intimacy with God and spiritual growth in the midst of trials, struggle, and hardship. What is a hardship you are facing right now and how are you responding?

4. **Read 1 Thessalonians 3:5–11.** What are signs of true Christian affection and care that you see modeled in this passage? What are practical ways we can grow in affection for others in the church family and how can we express this affection in ways that will bless them and honor God?

5. **Read 1 Thessalonians 3:12–13.** What are some of the indicators of forward progression in faith that are encouraged by Paul in this passage? What is one area you are growing in your faith and how is the journey of growth increasing your intimacy with God?

6. Tell about a person in your life who is an example of mature and consistent faith. How can you follow the example of this person and take a step forward in your Christian maturity? How can your group members pray for you as you seek to progress in this area of spiritual growth?

MEMORIZE

Each session, you will be given a key verse from the passage covered in the video teaching to memorize. This week, your memory verse is 1 Thessalonians 3:12:

> *May the Lord make your love increase and overflow for each other and for everyone else, just as ours does for you.*

Have everyone recite this verse out loud. Ask for any volunteers who would like to say the verse from memory.

RESPOND

What will you take away from this session? What is one practical next step you can take to move more fully into who God has created you to be?

PRAY

Close your group time by praying in any of the following directions:

- Thank God for the refining power of adversity and commit to embrace it even when it does not make sense.
- Ask God to help you extend care, kindness, and affection to other Christians he has placed in your life. Thank

him for specific people he has used to show you affection and love.

- Invite the Holy Spirit to help you make progress in your journey of faith and to propel you forward in spiritual maturity.
- Pray for a heart that beats and breaks for the people in your circles of influence who do not yet have faith in Jesus. Ask for strength to love them, serve them, pray for them, as well as courage to share the good news of Jesus as the Holy Spirit leads.

SESSION THREE

Reflect on the material you have covered in this session by engaging in the following between-session learning resources. This week, you will begin by reviewing a key verse to memorize for the session. During the next five days, you will have an opportunity to read a portion of 1 and 2 Thessalonians and an additional passage on the key themes of this session, reflect on what you learn, respond by taking action, journal some of your insights, and pray about what God has taught you. Finally, the last day, you will review the key verse and reflect on what you have learned for the week.

DAY 15

Memorize: Begin this week's personal study by reciting 1 Thessalonians 3:12:

> *May the Lord make your love increase and overflow for each other and for everyone else, just as ours does for you.*

Now try to say the verse from memory.

Reflect: Care, affection, and community. These are all things that every Christian is born for. This is part of your destiny both in this life and for eternity. What is a step forward you can take in showing godly affection and kindness to a Christian that God has placed in your life?

DAY 16

Read: 1 Thessalonians 3:1–4 and 2 Corinthians 11.

Reflect: Some Bible passages leave us smiling, happy, and immediately encouraged. Other Bible passages are sobering and deeply serious. Today's passages come in the second category. Suffering, trials, and even persecution are part of the Christian journey. They can't be avoided if we walk hand in hand with our suffering Savior. Why do you think times of pain and struggle are built into the Christian life and how do you feel when you realize that you were born for adversity?

Journal:
- What are some of the adverse situations you have faced in your Christian journey?
- How has God used these times to draw you closer to him and deepen your faith?

Pray: *Sovereign God, I dare to look back and thank you for how you have used times of adversity and affliction to bind my heart to yours and grow my trust in you.*

DAY 17

Read: 1 Thessalonians 3:1–4 and Acts 16:16–40.

Reflect: It is possible to walk closely with Jesus, follow his call, be in step with the Spirit, and still run into times of pain and persecution. What do you learn from watching the apostle Paul and his ministry partners as they faced very difficult times that came entirely because they were faithful to the call of Jesus?

Journal:
- What attitudes and actions marked the lives of Paul and his companions in the middle of difficult times?
- What challenging situations are you facing right now? How can you adjust your responses to adversity so that others can see the presence and power of Jesus alive in your life, even in the hard times?

Pray: Pray for power to respond with faith, hope, trust, and even joy in the midst of adversity.

DAY 18

Read: 1 Thessalonians 3:5–11 and 1 Corinthians 13.

Reflect: You were born for affection, care, and kindness. God has saved you and is at work in you. He is also working through you to show his great love and affection to people in your home, church, and the world around you. In 1 Thessalonians we see examples of true Christian love and care. In 1 Corinthians 13 we receive a road map for how Christians are to live in community with others. If you look at the picture of love in this passage, how could this guide the way you interact with Christians and non-believers in your life?

Journal:
- Consider the Christians in your life who have been great models of care and affection. How can you learn from their example as you seek to love others?
- What settings and circumstances do you have a hard time being caring and compassionate about and how can you adjust your actions and attitudes so that you are more affectionate?

Pray: *God of love, care, and tender affection, help me recognize that you have made me to extend your love to each person I encounter.* Pray for specific people you have a hard time being affectionate toward. Invite God to grow your heart and care for these people.

DAY 19

Read: 1 Thessalonians 3:12–13 and Hebrews 5:11–6:12.

Reflect: It breaks the heart of God when his children get stalled. Like a loving earthly parent, God wants to see his children thrive, grow, and progress in faith. When we are stuck or refuse to move forward, God is ready to give us a push forward so we can keep progressing in our faith. As you read the Hebrews passage, what did you notice about how one follower of Jesus was challenging and encouraging other Christians to keep growing and moving forward in maturity?

Journal:
- Who has been a major factor in your spiritual progress? What have they done to help you grow, keep you on track, and continually progress in faith? How would your life be different if God had not used this person to help you grow?
- When has God used you to help another person grow in faith? What are ways you can continue cheering them on, challenging them, and encouraging this person to grow more mature in faith?

Pray: Lift up prayers of thanks for the people God has used to help you grow up in faith. Invite God to use you more and more to help others make progress in their walk with Jesus.

DAY 20

Read: 1 Thessalonians 3:12–13 and Ephesians 4.

Reflect: The goal Paul sets before us is staggering: "Until we all reach unity in the faith and in the knowledge of the Son of God and become mature, attaining to the whole measure of the fulness of Christ" (Ephesians 4:13). *"The whole measure of the fulness of Christ."* Let this sink in! We are progressing toward full maturity in Jesus so that we look like him, love like him, and live like him. What steps do you need to take as you continue on this glorious upward journey of becoming more like the Savior?

Journal:
- What are three or four characteristics of Jesus (as he lived, walked on this earth, and ministered) that you would like to make progress in?
- What practical steps can you take in each of these areas that will help you grow to be more like your Lord and Savior?

Pray: Confess where you have stopped seeking to grow in Christlikeness. Ask for fresh power, commitment, and progress in these areas of faith development.

DAY 21

Memorize: Conclude this week's personal study by again reciting 1 Thessalonians 3:12:

May the Lord make your love increase and overflow for each other and for everyone else, just as ours does for you.

Reflect: Not only are Christians called to grow in our love for each other (fellow Jesus followers), but we are called to show affection and compassion on "everyone else." Focus on one person in your life who is not yet a Christian. How can you show God's affection to this person in the coming week?

MIND YOUR BUSINESS

1 THESSALONIANS 4:1–12

What should the followers of Jesus be doing every day from now until our Lord returns? We should be mindful of what God says matters the most. Faithful and mature followers of Jesus devote themselves to abounding in moral purity, relational health, and setting a godly example.

WELCOME

Imagine new parents teaching their little girl how to talk. For months they coax and cajole her. "Sweetie, can you say Mama? Mama!" "Honey, you can do it, say Daddy, Dada, can you say Dada?" Finally, after more than a thousand invitations to speak a first word, she looks up and says, "Dada!" Both parents hear it. They are thrilled. They are confident she actually spoke a word. They get her to say it again and this time they record it on video and send the record of this monumental moment to family and friends. Both dad and mom are confident their daughter is the brightest and most articulate child to grace planet earth. Their daughter spoke!

What do these delighted parents do next? Choose one of the options below.

a. They are perfectly happy with their daughter knowing one word and do nothing to help her continue developing her language skills.
b. They commit to teach her one new word every year with the hope that their daughter will master close to twenty words by her twentieth birthday.
c. They ramp up the learning process immediately and do all they can to teach their little girl new words every single day.

Every parent knows the answer is "C." When a loving and attentive mom sees her child growing and learning, she wants to accelerate the process. When a caring dad sees his son walk, he wants to help him learn to run. When a parent sees meaningful progress in any area of their child's life, they long to see more and more!

Our heavenly Father also takes delight when his children grow and take forward steps in maturity. When God sees us walk, he wants to help us run. When we learn to pray, the Spirit of God wants to help us go even deeper. When we learn to humbly help others like our servant-Savior, he wants to see us grow even more. A loving earthly parent wants to see their child grow more and more in every area of life. In the same way, our loving heavenly Father delights to help us grow more and more into the image of his beloved Son, Jesus.

SHARE

What are some of the ways an earthly parent helps their child grow up so they can become the person they are meant to be? How is this an act of love and care on the part of a parent?

WATCH

Play the video for session four. As you watch, use the following outline to record any thoughts, questions, or key points that stand out to you.

Mind your head

God challenges and even prunes us when he sees great potential in our lives

Time flies, so do your work, and abound more and more

Abound in **purity** (1 Thessalonians 4:3–8)

Even when you live in a sexually broken and promiscuous culture

Christians approach relationships differently than our culture

Our intimacy with God is impacted by how we mind our sexual desires

Life transformation comes *after* a person places their faith in Jesus

Abound in your **relationships** (1 Thessalonians 4:9–10)

Abound in your **example** (1 Thessalonians 4:11–12)

Let your life do the talking

A good example opens the door for the gospel

DISCUSS

Take a few minutes with your group members to discuss what you just watched and explore these concepts in Scripture. Use the following questions to help guide your discussion.

1. What impacted you the most as you watched Levi's teaching on 1 Thessalonians 4?

2. If you could make a sign warning modern Christians to be careful, watchful, and mindful of something that is a real and present danger in our world today, what would your sign say?

3. What ways does God prune and refine the lives of faithful and fruitful Christians so that we can bear even more fruit and shine more brightly for him?

4. **Read 1 Thessalonians 4:3–8.** Levi gave some examples of how the ancient Roman world was sexually perverse. The city of Thessalonica was a center of sexual cults and immoral activity. Why is it important for us to have a clear picture of the environment of Paul's ministry as we seek to abound in sexual purity in our world today? What is God's plan for sexual purity and how can we embrace it in our personal lives and help other Christians do the same?

5. **Read 1 Thessalonians 4:9–10.** To mind our relationships is to actively strengthen them, to take seriously the call to love people well, and to challenge other believers to grow in faith. What are specific ways you can mind your relationships with other Christians and make them even stronger for Jesus?

6. **Read 1 Thessalonians 4:11–12.** Paul implies that Christians who work hard at their vocation with quiet humility will become a witness to the world and have opportunities to tell others about the love and grace of Jesus. How have you seen or experienced this to be true?

7. The promise of the return of Jesus causes some Christians to get lazy, stop working, and not mind their business. Why should a bold confidence that Jesus will return someday cause us to work hard, serve faithfully, and strive to become more and more like Jesus in our vocational world?

MEMORIZE

Each session, you will be given a key verse from the passage covered in the video teaching to memorize. This week, your memory verse is 1 Thessalonians 4:1:

> *As for other matters, brothers and sisters, we instructed you how to live in order to please God, as in fact you are living. Now we ask you and urge you in the Lord Jesus to do this more and more.*

Have everyone recite this verse out loud. Ask for any volunteers who would like to say the verse from memory.

RESPOND

What will you take away from this session? What is one practical next step you can take to follow Jesus more closely than you have in the past?

PRAY

Close your group time by praying in any of the following directions:

- Pray for conviction and power to live in sexual purity. Ask God to help you grow in holiness and confess any struggles in this area.
- Ask God to help you abound in healthy relationships. Lift up places in your relational world that are broken and pray for God's healing and courage to do your part.
- Ask God to help you tend to your vocational world so that you are increasingly effective. Also, ask for God to help you work so diligently that others will notice and ask questions that will allow you to give witness to God's goodness and the grace of Jesus.

SESSION FOUR

Reflect on the material you have covered in this session by engaging in the following between-session learning resources. Each week, you will begin by reviewing the key verse to memorize for the session. During the next five days, you will have an opportunity to read a portion of 1 Thessalonians 4 and other passages of the Bible. Take time to reflect on what you learn, respond by taking action, journal some of your insights, and pray about what God has taught you. Finally, the last day, you will review the key verse and reflect on what you have learned for the week.

DAY 22

Memorize: Begin this week's personal study by reciting 1 Thessalonians 4:1:

> *As for other matters, brothers and sisters, we instructed you how to live in order to please God, as in fact you are living. Now we ask you and urge you in the Lord Jesus to do this more and more.*

Now try to say the verse from memory.

Reflect: We can bring pleasure to God when we grow up in faith. He delights for us to mirror the image of Jesus. Reflect on one area of your spiritual journey where you *have* been growing and thank God that you are taking steps forward. Think about an area you are stalled or moving backward on your faith journey and ask God to help you surrender this area of your life to him more fully with each passing day.

DAY 23

Read: 1 Thessalonians 4:1–2 and Colossians 3.

Reflect: The apostle Paul was comfortable urging others to grow in their faith. He cheered them on as they became more like Jesus. Think about two or three people in the Bible who were examples of faithfully following God. What did they do and how did they live out their faith? As you seek to urge others to walk closely with the Savior, what is one specific lesson you learn from a biblical character that you can share with those you are seeking to spur on toward growth in Christlikeness? Be aware! When the Spirit of God uses you to challenge others to grow deeper in their faith, he might just use them to do the same in your life.

Journal:

- Think of a Christian from church history who was an example of following Jesus faithfully. (You may want to look online or refer to a book or two.) What can you learn from the way that person lived their life?

- How can you take the lessons you have learned from mature spiritual mentors (people who have discipled you) and do the same with people who are younger than you in their faith?

Pray: Ask God to give you courage to challenge others to grow in faith and humility. Also listen and respond when God uses people to urge you toward spiritual growth.

DAY 24

Read: 1 Thessalonians 4:3–8 and Proverbs 5.

Reflect: The world is filled with sexual temptations. It was true in the days of Solomon, it was true in the world of the apostle Paul, and it is just as true today. The shape and form of the enticements might change with time, but the battle remains the same. Why do you think God is so concerned about his children avoiding sexual sin? What damage comes to our spiritual life, our relational life, and our emotional life when we wander into sexual disobedience? What are ways we can set up godly boundaries and warning systems in our life that will help us recognize when we are drifting toward sexual sin that compromises God's good plan for us as men and women?

Journal:
- What are some of the lures and enticements that the enemy uses with you when it comes to sexual temptation? How can you identify these and run from them before you end up in a compromising situation?
- What habits and behaviors lead you toward purity and holiness as a man or woman in our sex-saturated world? What steps forward can you take to adopt these kinds of habits in your daily life?

Pray: Pray for eyes to see when you are being enticed to compromise sexually. Ask the Spirit of God to give you power to reject these temptations, to run away if needed, and to develop habits that block out these temptations before they take root in your heart and life.

DAY 25

Read: 1 Thessalonians 4:9–10 and 1 John 3:11–18

Reflect: Love each other more and more! Just a little love is not enough. Even a lot of love is not enough. When Jesus was asked about the most important commandment of all, he was crystal clear that loving God and loving people should be the top concerns of a Christian. Paul was commending the Thessalonian Christians for their great love for each other. He praised them for loving all the Christians around Macedonia. Then he started urging again . . . love more and more! Who do you love that needs to be loved even more?

Journal:
- List three or four people you really love and care about. Write down at least one way you show love to each of these people.
- As you look at the names on your list and the ways you show them love, answer these questions: How do I step my love quotient up a notch? What is a way I could love them that would shock or surprise them?

Pray: Ask God for the courage, discipline, and power to take greater action of love toward the people you noted on your list.

DAY 26

Read: 1 Thessalonians 4:11–12 and Proverbs 6:1–19.

Reflect: When we hear the phrase "mind your business," we think of it as an exhortation to stop being nosy or too curious.

But the apostle Paul was really calling the Thessalonians to be mindful of the work God had for them to do and be diligent in fulfilling God's desire for them to work hard. The goal was that each person would provide for themselves through the work of their hands and even produce enough to help others. People who live this way catch the eye of the world and become a witness to the goodness and power of God.

Journal:

- What work has God called you to do: vocationally, in the community, in your home, and in the church?
- How can you pay closer attention to God's call for you to work hard and be diligent? What are ways you can honor God by working harder and keeping your mind focused on his call for your life?

Pray: Thank God for the dignity of the work he has given you and pray for discipline to work as hard as you can for the glory of Jesus.

DAY 27

Read: 1 Thessalonians 4:13–18 and Matthew 24.

Reflect: Jesus will return again. There is no question about it. One day, all that is wrong and broken will be made right. Until then, we need to be careful that we don't get caught up in silly speculation, anxious anticipation, or laziness. The certain return of Jesus is not a reason to put our life in neutral and just hang out until the end. Just the opposite. A firm and confident theology of Jesus's second coming should launch us into a life of faithfulness, hard work, and bold gospel sharing. What is your outlook on the return of Jesus? Does it inspire you to diligent service and passionate faithfulness? This is exactly what Jesus has in mind.

Journal:
- What should you be doing with increasing commitment as you live for Jesus between today and his second coming? What areas in your spiritual growth have you let slip to the back burner but need to get more of your attention and action?
- What specific actions do you need to take in your life that will make you prepared, on a daily basis, for the return of Jesus?

Pray: Ask for courage to admit and name the things you have ignored in your spiritual growth journey. Pray for power to take a next step of growth in one of these areas . . . starting today.

DAY 28

Memorize: Conclude this week's personal study by again reciting 1 Thessalonians 4:1:

> *As for other matters, brothers and sisters, we instructed you how to live in order to please God, as in fact you are living. Now we ask you and urge you in the Lord Jesus to do this more and more.*

Reflect: A "more and more" lifestyle is one that never settles. This kind of outlook drives a Christian to always hunger for more of God's Word, to always pray with deeper passion, to always give with increasing joy and generosity, to always serve with growing frequency and humility . . . you get the picture. Think about how your life could change if you committed to always seek for more and more of what God has planned for your life. Make this a matter of prayer in the coming week.

BETWEEN NOW AND THEN

1 THESSALONIANS 5:12–28

Jesus will return in glory and power . . . Christians are confident of this truth. The big question is, what are we to do as we await his second coming? The apostle Paul was clear that faithful followers of Jesus will use the time between now and the return of our Savior (or when we go to Jesus) to honor people and God in every way possible. Our waiting is not passive complacency but faithful living.

WELCOME

Our life is filled with moments of waiting between the now and then.

Now I am too young to drive a car; *then* I will get my license and have freedom.

Now I am single; *then* I will get married, have a family, and settle down.

Now I am in school; *then* I will finish my degree and start my career.

Now I am working; *then* I will be able to retire and finally relax.

Now I am living in this body on this planet; *then* I will see Jesus face-to-face and walk with him in glory!

In the days of Jesus, many people were so ready to get to their heavenly *then* that they treated their lives *now* as a distraction and a hurdle to jump over as soon as possible. Through the history of the church, groups of Christians have become so consumed with the eternal that they forgot to live for Jesus every day until the end of their lives. It is still a temptation for many Christians to, as the old saying goes, be "so heavenly minded they are no earthly good!"

God wants us to look forward to heaven but fully engage in the life he has given us on this earth. Enjoy the flavor of a good ice cream cone on a hot summer day. Delight in the energy of your dog running, jumping, and licking your nose. Embrace the blessing of great friendships. Revel in a wonder of passionate worship in the community of God's people. Serve Jesus and his people with deep humility. Follow the mission God has given you every day of your life from *now* until *then*!

SHARE

What are some of the potential dangers we can encounter if a Christian fixates on heaven but does not seek to live fully for Jesus each day of their life?

WATCH

Play the video for session five. As you watch, use the following outline to record any thoughts, questions, or key points that stand out to you.

Story . . . When you have no idea what is in your hands

Review . . . Know what the Bible teaches about the end of time because incorrect information leads to unnecessary fear

When did grief first enter your life?

What are we called to do between now and then?

Don't focus so much on what is next that we miss what God has for us now

Know your assignment between now and then

Don't get obsessed with what we can't understand and were not meant to understand

Honor Up (1 Thessalonians 5:12–13)

Honor Down (1 Thessalonians 5:14)

Honor All Around (1 Thessalonians 5:15–18)

Honor God (1 Thessalonians 5:19–22)

DISCUSS

Take a few minutes with your group members to discuss what you just watched and explore these concepts in Scripture. Use the following questions to help guide your discussion.

I. What impacted you the most as you watched Levi's teaching on 1 Thessalonians 5?

2. What is a biblical truth about the end of time that you have learned from your reading of 1 and 2 Thessalonians, and how can this truth impact how you live from now until that day comes?

3. **Read 1 Thessalonians 5:12–13.** What are practical ways we can bless, uplift, and encourage church leaders and people in roles of authority in the church, homes, and society? What is a specific action your small group can take together to live out this exhortation to honor upward?

4. **Read 1 Thessalonians 5:14.** Who are some groups of people in your church or community who are struggling, disheartened, or weak, and what are ways you could honor them? What is a specific action your small group can take together to live out this exhortation to honor downward?

5. **Read 1 Thessalonians 5:15–18.** What are ways you can honor God everywhere you go and at all times in *one* of the following ways?
    ◦ By rejoicing with authentic passion . . .
    ◦ By praying with faith and confidence in God . . .
    ◦ By expressing words of thanks no matter what you face . . .

    How can this kind of faith and behavior be a witness to the world that God is present and good?

6. **Read 1 Thessalonians 5:19–28.** By what attitudes and actions can we seek to keep our spirit, soul, and body blameless in the time between now and when we see Jesus face-to-face? How does our commitment to live a blameless life bring honor to God?

MEMORIZE

Each session, you will be given a key verse (or verses) to memorize from the passage covered in the video teaching. This week, your memory verses are 1 Thessalonians 5:16–18:

> [16] *Rejoice always,* [17] *pray continually,* [18] *give thanks in all circumstances; for this is God's will for you in Christ Jesus.*

Have everyone recite these verses out loud. Ask for any volunteers who would like to say these verses from memory.

RESPOND

What will you take away from this session? What is one practical next step you can take to live in a way that honors up, down, or all around?

PRAY

Close your group time by praying in any of the following directions:

- Ask God to bless and strengthen the leaders he has placed in your life. Lift up people by name and pray for God's protection and hand to be on them.
- Invite the Holy Spirit to soften your heart toward those you encounter who are broken, weak, hurting, and

marginalized. Commit to do what you can to bless and honor these people when God opens your eyes to see their needs.

- Lift up prayers that honor God, recognize his goodness, and praise him for who he is.

SESSION FIVE

Reflect on the material you have covered in this session by engaging in the following between-session learning resources. Each week, you will begin by reviewing the key verses to memorize for the session. During the next five days, you will have an opportunity to read a portion of 1 Thessalonians 5, reflect on what you learn, respond by taking action, journal some of your insights, and pray about what God has taught you. Finally, the last day, you will review the key verses and reflect on what you have learned for the week.

DAY 29

Memorize: Begin this week's personal study by reciting 1 Thessalonians 5:16–18:

> [16] *Rejoice always,* [17] *pray continually,* [18] *give thanks in all circumstances; for this is God's will for you in Christ Jesus.*

Now try to say the verses from memory.

Reflect: There are some actions Christians should engage in at all times and every moment of their lives. No matter what we face or where we are, rejoicing honors our God because he is always good. With every breath we take, we can talk with God. He is always near and longs to hear from his children. Thankfulness can be expressed no matter what we are experiencing. Which of these practices comes most naturally to you? How can you increase this in your daily life?

DAY 30

Read: 1 Thessalonians 5:1–11 and 1 Corinthians 15.

Reflect: We just don't know. We can't know. Jesus was clear about this. No matter how many books are written to prognosticate about when Jesus will return, we simply can't predict it. So, we live every day prepared to meet Jesus and ready to live another day for him. We don't doze off (literally or figuratively) but stay sober and attentive to the will of our Lord. This is really a beautiful picture! We are ever ready to meet the Lord and always prepared to live for him for as long as we are on this earth. What does it look like to live each day as one who is ready for Jesus' return at any moment? What does it look like to rise each day with an excitement to live fully for the risen Savior?

Journal:
- Consider one or two ways you can be more prepared to meet Jesus if he were to return today or if your life were to end?

• What is *one* way you can prepare to live for Jesus in the coming year, knowing that he might not return for years, decades, or centuries?

Pray: Pray for a healthy balance of being ever prepared to meet Jesus and just as ready to live the next decade for him.

DAY 31

Read: 1 Thessalonians 5:12–13 and 1 Samuel 24.

Reflect: All of us have those in roles of authority over us, whether family members, governing authorities, work supervisors, teachers, church leaders, and so on. We do not have to do everything they tell us—our allegiance to Jesus far outweighs our commitment to any person—but God's Word clearly teaches us to honor upward. We need to look for ways to show respect and kindness to these people. Who has God placed in authority over you and how can you begin praying for them?

Journal:
- Who are people with a role of authority in your life and whom you really trust and respect? What can you do to honor, encourage, and bless these people?
- Think of a person who has a role of authority over you, but you have a hard time honoring them. How can you pray for this person and encourage them in a small way that helps you start a journey of appropriate respect?

Pray: Ask God to give you courage to show respect and honor to people who are placed over you, even when you find this hard to do. Ask for the wisdom of the Holy Spirit to help you see the best way to show honor to these individuals.

DAY 32

Read: 1 Thessalonians 5:14 and John 13.

Reflect: One of the most powerful pictures of honoring downward is when Jesus, God in human flesh, knelt and washed the dirty feet of his disciples. When he got to Thomas, who would later doubt him, Jesus humbly cleaned his feet. When the Savior came to Peter, who would soon deny that he knew him, Jesus served. When he got to Judas, who would betray him, the Lord of glory, served like a household slave. When he had finished washing every foot at the table, Jesus called his disciples to do the same . . . every day of their lives. If you ever feel you are above honoring downward, just remember that Jesus would have washed your feet had you been at that table.

Journal:

- Create a brief list of people that God has placed in your life needing you to increase your willingness to honor downward and serve them?
- What makes it hard for you to serve with humility . . . in particular those over whom you have a role of authority? How can you take a next step into daily service and honor the people God has placed in your life?

Pray: Ask God to open your eyes to look downward and notice people who need care, love, and acts of service. Then, ask God to give you courage and commitment to honor down.

DAY 33

Read: 1 Thessalonians 5:15–18 and Philippians 4.

Reflect: It is easy to identify those we need to honor up toward. We can also quickly identify people we can honor down to.

What does it look like to honor all around? This is living with a perpetual awareness that every moment is a chance to extend honor, blessing, and kindness. It is about keeping our eyes and heart open to opportunities that present themselves in the flow of life. The Thessalonians were called to share joy, lift up prayers, and express thankfulness. The Philippian church was called to let everyone see their gentleness and to be generous. The picture is clear; we can and should seek to honor every person we meet.

Journal:
- What are some places you go in a normal week that you have never really seen as opportunities to be a person who blesses, honors, and encourages others?
- What actions could you take in the coming week to be a conduit of God's goodness, kindness, and blessing in these places? Be specific about where you will be and how you could honor people.

Pray: Ask the Holy Spirit to help you tune in to the needs of the people around you as you walk through your week. Pray for courage and strength to speak and live in ways that honor people everywhere you go. This will change your life and bless people more than you can imagine.

DAY 34

Read: 1 Thessalonians 5:19–28 three times.

Reflect: This short passage could easily be an eight-week sermon series. As Paul finishes this Spirit-inspired letter, he gives a series of closing exhortations with rapid-fire power. Be responsive to the movement of the Holy Spirit. Honor prophetic ministry. Hold tight to all that is good. Turn your back on any and every kind of evil. The list goes on. Which of these do you need to hear and embrace with an open heart? As you read these words over and over, which one jumped out at you, or maybe irritated you because you don't want to hear it?

Journal:
- As you meditate on this passage, focus on one or two exhortations that you know God wants you to make a reality in your life.
- What are steps you can take to grow in one or two of these areas? With whom can you share your goal with and ask to prayerfully support this next step on your spiritual journey?

Pray: Pray about the one area from this passage that you would most like to avoid and forget about because it really challenges you. Ask God to keep convicting you and give you strength to follow his will in this area of your life.

DAY 35

Memorize: Conclude this week's personal study by again reciting 1 Thessalonians 5:16–18:

> *16 Rejoice always, 17 pray continually, 18 give thanks in all circumstances; for this is God's will for you in Christ Jesus.*

Reflect: These three invitations are massive! Paul does not just encourage us to rejoice but to do it at all times. He not only calls us to pray but to do it in a continual manner. We are not just to be thankful but to find things we are thankful for in every situation of life. Which of these three is most challenging for you and what is a next step forward you can take to help you honor God in the flow of your life?

KEEP CALM AND CARRY ON

2 THESSALONIANS

A short time after writing the first letter to the church in Thessalonica, the Apostle Paul got word that the Christians in that church were not responding and taking his teaching seriously. Inspired by the Holy Spirit, Paul wrote a second letter to the same church and repeated many of the same teachings and warnings. One of the biggest themes was for believers to keep pressing into the will of God, even in hard times. He called them to stay calm and keep following Jesus no matter what they faced!

WELCOME

"Don't bury your head in the sand like an ostrich."
"He froze like a deer in the headlights."

Which of these two animal-based colloquialisms comes from accurate information about the animal being used as an illustration? Here are the facts. Ostriches don't bury their heads in the sand. What they do is bury their eggs in holes in the ground, and several times a day they poke their head in to turn the eggs. On the other hand, when a deer steps into a road at night and looks toward an oncoming car, if the beam of the headlights hit eyes that are fully dilated, the deer can't see at all and will often freeze until their eyes adjust. If it takes too long for the deer to recognize what is happening, it's bad news for the deer and the car.

Inaction, freezing, refusing to move can be very costly. When a person panics, they often experience paralysis. This can be very dangerous. If someone is driving on a wet, slick, or icy road and their back wheels go into a slide, panicking can make things worse quickly. What needs to happen is a calm response that allows the person to gently steer into the skid . . . the same direction the wheels are sliding. It might seem counterintuitive, but this calm action can help a person avoid an accident and maybe save lives.

Even the Bible includes accounts of fear leading to paralysis. After Jesus died on the cross and was buried, guards were posted at the tomb to protect the body. An angel of God came down from heaven and the guards were so terrified that they literally froze like dead men (see Matthew 28:2–4). Panic can lead to paralysis.

As Paul wrote to the church in Thessalonica, he knew they were facing persecution. Fear was beginning to take hold. They were spiritually frozen and paralyzed. They stopped following Jesus with the joy and passion that had marked their earlier faith. The message from God for this young church is one we still need to hear today.

Don't be afraid. Don't panic. Don't freeze.

Instead, be calm and press on.

SHARE

Tell about a time you became fearful, worried, or were so surprised that you panicked or froze. What was the result of this situation?

or

Tell about a time when you had a sense of "calm in a storm" and were able to press forward even though it was a tough situation.

WATCH

Play the video for session six. As you watch, use the following outline to record any thoughts, questions, or key points that stand out to you.

Stand Firm . . . A story of resolute courage

2 Thessalonians, a rebroadcasting of 1 Thessalonians:

Remember Paul's story and transformation

Remember the setting of the city of Thessalonica

The reason for this second letter . . . the same problems persist

Our greatest mistakes can come in our areas of perceived strength

A reminder, reiteration, rebroadcast:

Grace and peace (1 Thessalonians 1:1–2)

The problem of persecution (1 Thessalonians 1:3–4)

The wisdom of Paul's leadership . . . praise what you want repeated

The second coming of Jesus . . . don't get confused

Jesus is coming back

No one knows when

Live holy lives and keep sharing your faith

DISCUSS

Take a few minutes with your group members to discuss what you just watched and explore these concepts in Scripture. Use the following questions to help guide your discussion.

1. What impacted you the most as you watched Levi's teaching on 2 Thessalonians?

2. **Read 2 Thessalonians 1:5–7.** One thing that helps us stay calm and press on when times are hard is knowing the truth and holding on to it. There are at least five declarations of truth in these three verses. What are they and how can embracing each truth give us peace and strength to keep following Jesus?

3. **Read 2 Thessalonians 1:11–12.** Paul offers a brief but powerful prayer for Christians enduring suffering, persecution, or hardship. How can we adopt these same focal points as we pray for the needs of others (and our own needs) in such times? What could happen if God were to answer these specific prayers?

4. **Read 2 Thessalonians 2:13–17.** What do our lives look like when we stand firm and hold to the teaching of God's Word? How do our lives change when we give up on following God's Word and trust in our own wisdom or the ways of this world?

5. **Read 2 Thessalonians 3:6–10.** Paul addressed the issue of idleness in 1 Thessalonians, but now he really dials it up! What is the biblical teaching for how Christians and the church should deal with people who are lazy and refuse to work (when they are fully capable)? Why are we reluctant to do this, and why should we press past our fears and love people enough to call them out of their idleness?

6. **Read 2 Thessalonians 3:1–5.** We are to pray that the message of our Lord would spread rapidly and be honored by those who hear it. What can you do in your personal life to spread the message of Jesus where you live, work, and recreate? How can your group members keep you accountable to engage in sharing the gospel with people in your life who still need to know Jesus?

MEMORIZE

Each session, you will be given a key verse from the passage covered in the video teaching to memorize. This week, your memory verse is 2 Thessalonians 2:15:

So then, brothers and sisters, stand firm and hold fast to the teachings we passed on to you, whether by word of mouth or by letter.

Have everyone recite these verses out loud. Ask for any volunteers who would like to say the verse from memory.

RESPOND

What will you take away from this session? What is one practical next step you can take to live with a calm spirit and keep pressing into what God has planned for you?

PRAY

Close your group time by praying in any of the following directions:

- Ask God to help you pinpoint an area where you have given up and backed off what you know is honoring to Jesus. Pray for a renewed commitment to be attentive to this area of your spiritual life and for boldness to take steps of growth in the coming days.
- Just as the Spirit moved Paul to repeat some of the same messages and lessons for the Christians in Thessalonica, God continually prompts us to repent, change, and follow him—whether through the Scriptures, a godly friend, a timely sermon, or internal nudging. As God does

this, pray for power to turn away from sin and toward holiness.

- Pray for your group members to refrain from fear, worry, or spiritual paralysis and ask God to fill them with calm that will free them to press on toward his will for their lives.

SESSION SIX

Reflect on the material you have covered in this session by engaging in the following between-session learning resources. Each week, you will begin by reviewing the key verse to memorize for the session. During this week, you will have an opportunity to read 2 Thessalonians, reflect on what you learn, respond by taking action, journal some of your insights, and pray about what God has taught you. Finally, the last day, you will review the key verse and reflect on what you have learned for the week.

DAY 36

Memorize: Begin this week's personal study by reciting 2 Thessalonians 2:15:

> So then, brothers and sisters, stand firm and hold fast to the teachings we passed on to you, whether by word of mouth or by letter.

Now try to say the verse from memory.

Reflect: How is your posture? Are you standing up, living confidently, firm in your faith? We are called to stand firm and not let anything blow us over. Stand firm in your daily relationship with Jesus. Stand firm against the enticements of the enemy. Stand firm in your theological convictions. Stand firm in a lifestyle of holiness. Where is the wind blowing hard against you and what can you do to make sure you stand firm in this area of your life?

DAY 37

Read: 2 Thessalonians 1.

Reflect: We are invited to pray with consistent passion and faith. What will it look like for you to pray:

That you and other Christians would live lives worthy of God's calling,

That you and the believers you know would see every good desire in your heart become a reality,

That the name of our Lord (his person and character) would be glorified in your group members,

That we would be glorified in Jesus.

Journal:

- What are you thankful for as you think of the members of your small group and the experience you had walking through this study together?
- What prayer needs have you gathered for each person in your group over these six sessions and how can you keep these on the front burner of your heart over the coming weeks?

Pray: Pray for the needs your group members have shared with each other over the past weeks together.

DAY 38

Read: 2 Thessalonians 2.

Reflect: Paul warns the Christians in Thessalonica that they should not be unsettled or caught up in all the false teachings about the end times. The reality of Jesus' second coming is not meant to cause fear and inaction. Just the opposite, it is meant to gives us a calm confidence that we know how the story ends so we can live for Jesus every single day until he returns or we go to be with him. What are some of the current teachings and movements that overemphasize the end times and cause a distraction rather than help Christians live for Jesus with faithful devotion? (Every generation has these.)

Journal:

- What kind of end times teaching keeps Christians from engaging in the world and living each day for Jesus? How can you be careful to avoid these?
- What kind of teaching about the second coming of Jesus gives a healthy and balanced outlook that makes believers calm and helps them live each day for Jesus? How can you lean into healthy views of the end times and be more prepared to follow Jesus faithfully today?

Pray: Ask God to give you discernment when it comes to those who speak, write about, or post blogs and articles about the end times. Pray that you will never get so enamored by questionable teachings that they keep you from walking intimately with your Savior today.

DAY 39

Read: 2 Thessalonians 3.

Reflect: Good biblical theology leads Christians to be hard workers who not only pay their own bills but are able to be generous toward God and people in need. Paul comes down hard on those who are so focused on the second coming of Jesus that they stop working and expect everyone else to take care of them. We are called to be busy doing what honors God and not busybodies who run around and get others riled up. What are ways you need to get busy serving Jesus and working hard at your vocation?

Journal:
- What are signs that a person is busy serving Jesus, working hard, and basing their life on solid biblical theology?
- What are indicators of a person who has become a busybody whose theology (particularly about the second coming of Jesus) has gotten off track?

Pray: Pray for diligence and commitment to work hard and never get off track in your beliefs such that you would dishonor God by becoming lazy and dependent on the hard work of others.

DAY 40

Memorize: Conclude your forty-day personal study by again reciting 2 Thessalonians 2:15:

So then, brothers and sisters, stand firm and hold fast to the teachings we passed on to you, whether by word of mouth or by letter.

Now try to say this verse completely from memory.

Reflect: Not only are we to stand firm but we are to hold fast to the teaching we have received. Many areas of biblical teaching are being challenged from outside (and sometimes inside) of the church. We are expected to hold fast to what the Bible teaches us. Hold fast to the teaching that calls us to compassion, service, and humility. Hold fast to the moral and sexual standards the Bible sets for human flourishing. Hold fast to the call to share the good news of Jesus with a gracious heart and a relentless devotion. Hold fast to the call to generosity and joyful sharing of what God has placed in our hands. Where has your grip loosened and how can you hold fast to God's Word with fresh conviction?

LEADER'S GUIDE

Thank you for your willingness to lead your group through this study! What you have chosen to do is valuable and will make a great difference in the lives of others. The rewards of being a leader are different from those of participating, and we hope that as you lead you will find your own walk with Jesus deepened by this experience.

This study on 1 and 2 Thessalonians in the *40 Days Through the Book* series is built around video content and small-group interaction. As the group leader, think of yourself as the host. Your job is to take care of your guests by managing the behind-the-scenes details so that when everyone arrives, they can enjoy their time together. As the leader, your role is not to answer all the questions or reteach the content—the video and study guide will do that work. Your role is to guide the experience and cultivate your group into a teaching community. This will make it a place for members to process, question, and reflect on the teaching.

Before your first meeting, make sure everyone has a copy of the study guide. This will keep everyone on the same page and help the process run more smoothly. If members are unable to purchase the guide, arrange it so they can share with other members. Giving everyone access to the material will position this study to be as rewarding as possible. Everyone should feel free to write in his or her study guide and bring it to group every week.

SETTING UP THE GROUP

Your group will need to determine how long you want to meet each week so you can plan your time accordingly. Generally, most groups like to meet for either sixty minutes or ninety minutes, so you could use one of the following schedules:

SECTION	60 MINUTES	90 MINUTES
WELCOME (members arrive and get settled)	5 minutes	5 minutes
SHARE (discuss one of the opening questions for the session)	5 minutes	10 minutes
READ (discuss the questions based on the Scripture reading for the session)	5 minutes	10 minutes
WATCH (watch the video teaching material together and take notes)	15 minutes	15 minutes
DISCUSS (discuss the Bible study questions based on the video teaching)	25 minutes	40 minutes
RESPOND/PRAY (reflect on the key insights, pray together, and dismiss)	5 minutes	10 minutes

As the group leader, you will want to create an environment that encourages sharing and learning. A church sanctuary or formal classroom may not be as ideal as a living room, because those locations can feel formal and less intimate. No matter what setting you choose, provide enough comfortable seating for everyone, and, if possible, arrange the seats in a semicircle so everyone can see the video easily. This will make the transition between the video and group conversation more efficient and natural.

Also, try to get to the meeting site early so you can greet participants as they arrive. Simple refreshments create a welcoming atmosphere and can be a wonderful addition to a group study. Try to take food and pet allergies into account to make your guests as comfortable as possible. You may also want to consider offering childcare to couples with children who want to attend. Finally, be sure your media technology is working properly. Managing these details up front will make the rest of your group experience flow smoothly and provide a welcoming space in which to engage the content of this study on the letters to the Thessalonians.

STARTING THE GROUP TIME

Once everyone has arrived, it is time to begin the study. Here are some simple tips to make your group time healthy, enjoyable, and effective.

Begin the meeting with a short prayer and remind the group members to put their phones on silent. This is a way to make sure you can all be present with one another and with God. Next, give each person a few minutes to respond to the questions in the "Share" section. This won't require as much time in session one, but beginning in session two, people may need more time to share their insights from their personal studies. Usually, you won't answer the discussion questions yourself, but you should go first with the "Share" questions, answering briefly and with a reasonable amount of transparency.

At the end of session one, invite the group members to complete the "Your 40-Day Journey" for that week. Explain that they can share any insights the following week before the video teaching. Let them know it's not a problem if they can't get to these activities some weeks. It will still be beneficial for them to hear from the other participants in the group.

LEADING THE DISCUSSION TIME

Now that the group is engaged, watch the video and respond with some directed small-group discussion. Encourage the group members to participate in the discussion, but make sure they know this is not mandatory for the group, so as to not make them feel pressured to come up with an answer. As the discussion progresses, follow up with comments such as, "Tell me more about that," or, "Why did you answer that way?" This will allow the group participants to deepen their reflections and invite a meaningful conversation in a nonthreatening way.

Note that you have been given multiple questions to use in each session, and you do not have to use them all or even follow them in order. Feel free to pick and choose questions based on the needs of your group or how the conversation is flowing. Also, don't be afraid of silence. Offering a question and allowing up to thirty seconds of silence is okay. This space allows people to think about how they want to respond and gives them time to do so.

As group leader, you are the boundary keeper for your group. Do not let anyone (yourself included) dominate the group time. Keep an eye out for group members who might be tempted to "attack" folks they disagree with or try to "fix" those having struggles. These kinds of behaviors can derail a group's momentum, so they need to be steered in a different direction. Model active listening and encourage everyone in your group to do the same. This will make your group time a safe space and create a positive community.

The group discussion leads to a closing time of individual reflection and prayer. Encourage the participants to review what they have learned and write down their thoughts to the "Respond" section. Close by taking a few minutes to pray as directed as a group.

Thank you again for taking the time to lead your group. You are making a difference in the lives of others and having an impact on the kingdom of God!

Study Books of the Bible with Trusted Pastors

The 40 Days Through the Book series has been designed to help believers more actively engage with God's Word. Each study encourages participants to read through one book in the New Testament at least once during the course of 40 days and provides them with:

- A clear understanding of the background and culture in which the book was written,

- Insights into key passages of Scripture, and

- Clear applications and takeaways from the particular book that participants can apply to their lives.

Available now at your favorite bookstore, or streaming video on StudyGateway.com.

HarperChristian Resources

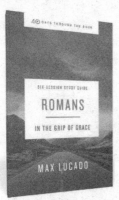

ROMANS
In The Grip Of Grace

Max Lucado

MARK
The Cost Of Discipleship

Jeff Manion

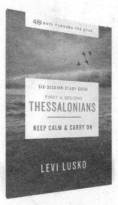

THESSALONIANS
Keep Calm & Carry On

Levi Lusko

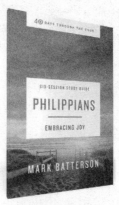

PHILIPPIANS
Embracing Joy

Mark Batterson

Also available from Jennie Lusko

Book
9780785232148

Study Guide
9780310112488

DVD with Free Streaming Access
9780310112501

Just like some plants need darkness to grow, many of us grow stronger in our faith in the dark and difficult times. It is in the sacred space of pain and promise that we begin to flourish.

In this six-session video Bible study, Jennie Lusko offers biblical hope in your struggles through personal and vulnerable examples of God not only helping her survive the darkness but thrive in it. Fighting and flourishing are meant to blend together, wherever you are.

Available now at your favorite bookstore,
or streaming video on StudyGateway.com.

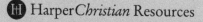